Infinite Nothingness

Devadipta Das

notionpress.com

INDIA • SINGAPORE • MALAYSIA

ISBN
Paperback 979-8-89777-648-1
Hardcase 979-8-89929-854-7

Contents

Forward

*I*n an age defined by fleeting attention spans and endless distractions, literature faces a paradoxical challenge: how to distill profundity into brevity without sacrificing depth. This collection, *Infinite Nothingness,* seeks to answer that call—a bold experiment in what I term "flash literature." Each piece within these pages is crafted to provoke extreme emotions, ignite intellectual curiosity, and reflect the complexities of existence—all while using very few words.

This is not a book to be read in one sitting; it is a book to be pondered. Let each reflection sink in, for in the brevity lies the depth, and in the depth lies the infinite

As you journey through *Infinite Nothingness,* let each piece serve as a portal to deeper truths about identity, meaning, love, suffering, and the cosmos.

And remember: the answers lie not outside but within you. May this collection disturb and enlighten, provoke and inspire. For those who dare to confront the infinite nothingness within themselves, there awaits a universe of discovery.

Welcome to the edge of thought. Welcome to *Infinite Nothingness.*

Light & Dark

It is so strange that anything that burns produces light.

Maybe that's what beauty really is?

The divine light is everywhere.

But the universe is wearing the mask of darkness.

Yes- too much darkness is scary.

But too much light will make you blind.

No doubt fire gives you light.

But it has the potential to burn you.

And the brightest lights end in the form of ashes.

The only difference between the light and the dark is the ability of vision.

The Mirror

The universe is the mirror of our thoughts and actions.

What a weird world we have created,

Here being good is considered a weakness,

Yet all we seek is goodness.

Lost to be found

I lost myself amidst all the chaos in the world;

Only to find myself back in solitude.

But that is where I fell in love!

With myself and with the world- there we became one!

For, in solitude lies the true test of personality.

Children are our desperate attempt at immortality.

But seldom do we realize that the continuity has end
and beginning imbibed within itself.

Why are you so sad while the cosmos that you are in is always dancing?

Beauty of the Beast

In a world where everyone is busy finding flaws in others,

Be someone who sees beauty even in beasts.

For if you find something beautiful or ugly,

It is actually the reflection of your inner reality.

Yes, if you give you shall get!

But if you give with the only intention of getting, you
shall never get.

Kindness is a virtue that helps one endure suffering.

Because God is kind to those who are kind to others.

Lies Sell

It takes a lot of courage to face the truth.

It is a fact that civilization is built on a pyramid of comforting lies.

For the truth is boring. The truth is empty.

But lies are interesting! Lies sell.

Courage is the ability to stand by what is right, to stand by what is true even when everyone around you thinks otherwise.

The world would have been lot easier if everything
was just black and white.

Yet, it would have been boring.

So we are lucky that the world is so colorful.

Yes! Beauty lies in the eyes of the beholder.

Yet, it is not a privilege.

It is a responsibility.

Freedom

Ode on Suffering

Let everyone suffer,

But let them suffer happily.

At least let them choose how they suffer.

Because to exist is to suffer.

But to live is to choose how you suffer,

And that is freedom,

That is happiness.

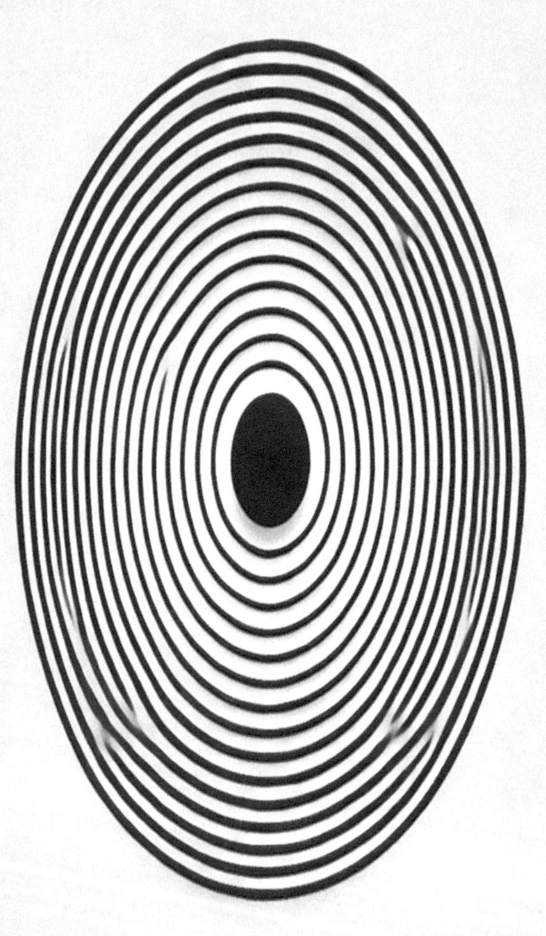

What you think you become,

What you become you radiate,

What you radiate others absorb.

Indeed, you have the power to change the world.

Are we doomed?

Satre said, 'Human beings are doomed to be free.'

I don't think so! Rather, human beings are free to be doomed.

The irony of this world is that most of the wars in
history have been fought in the name of men who gave
up their own lives for the sake of humanity.

It's so strange that sometimes the only way towards
peace is war.

I can define existence in merely three words- a big mystery.

But this is the irony; most people are ignorant that they are ignorant.

Our egos does not let us know that our knowledge is limited.

For knowledge begins and ends with the cognizance of ignorance.

We are so busy looking for magic everywhere else that we often forget that-

Existence is the greatest magic.

To be happy is to be truly free.

It is a fact of life that the most beautiful things will be abused the most.

The best ideas will be used to oppress the most.

The concept of God will be used the most in wars.

And love will be used to deceive the most.

If all of tragedy is nothing but comedy misunderstood;

All of existence is nothing but a divine comedy.

What a world we have inherited!

We are free to give meaning to existence.

Education was meant to set us free.

But ironically, it has made us slaves of our own minds.

Politics is the highest of all sciences and greatest of all arts.

There is no greater freedom than the freedom to give meaning to your own life.

The ability to exercise that freedom is happiness.

It is the greatest comedy to believe immortality to be a boon. Yet it is the birth of all tragedy.

The Universe

Flying and falling are like two sides of the same coin.

In order to fly one must be massless and objects in free-fall do not experience mass.

The eternal oneness in true form only exists in the form of nothingness.

The universe is a blank canvas waiting to be painted
by our colors.

Sometimes I want time to freeze.

Sometimes I want time to race.

I guess it's best that time passes at a constant pace.

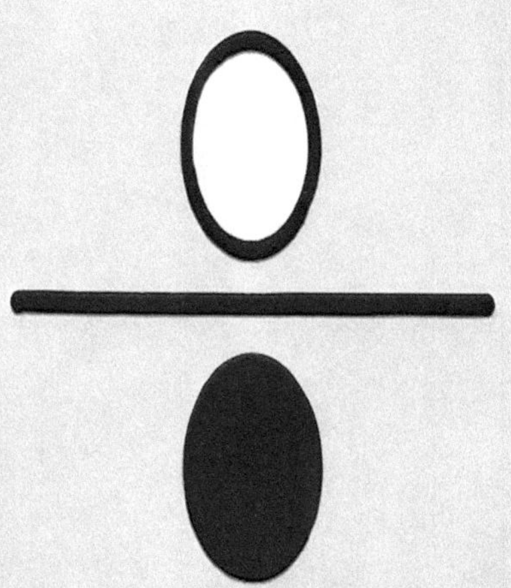

Time doesn't reflect change, it actually reflects continuity.

For the change is continuous.

Universe is a circle.

And a circle has no beginning or end.

In terms of pure mathematics and physics, the 'now' does not exist. But we all know that it does. I guess that is the beauty of 'now'. It exists in the realm of consciousness.

<u>Infinite...</u>

Everything you can imagine exists.

And whatever you can't imagine now, someday you will.

Creation is perfectly imperfect.

In the absence of gravity falling and flying are one and the same.

'I'- the Ego

We are not born with identity. We assume our identity through our experience. And our sense of identity changes based on our experiences.

Know Thyself

That is all you need to know.

And that is all there is to know.

<u>Incomplete?</u>

It is true that I am incomplete without everything else
in the universe.

But it is also true that 'Everything' is incomplete
without 'Me'.

And this in-itself is eternal.

Falling stars are always beautiful.

Until they are falling on you.

<u>The Stairway to Heaven</u>

Contrary to popular belief, the road to heaven goes
through hell.

Because in order to reach heaven, one has to first burn
through hell.

All of history is the history of identity struggle.

Who am I? Or what is the meaning of existence?

Why am I? Or what is the purpose of existence?

God is constantly trying to speak to us.

That is why thoughts exist.

The cessation of desire is also a desire,

The attempt to control desire is also a desire,

The goal is to be unaffected by desire, not to get rid of
it.

All the beginning and end of knowledge is in knowing that- I don't know. But I can know!

And to live is to attempt to know.

I am nothing. Yet I can be anything.

Everything is within me.

But I am nothing.

The Dark Truth

There is something intriguing about darkness.

It seems as if it is trying to whisper the truth.

Yet we all are too scared to face it.

It is true that too much pain will result in death.

But pain in the right proportion will only make you stronger.

I am the language the universe is writing itself with.

And so are you!

You are not what you think you are.

You are what you do in the pursuit of becoming the
person who you think you are.

*I want to stare at death right in the eyes and laugh
hysterically..., right before dying.*

You are the entire universe.

At the same time, you don't even matter.

Everything I think about myself is ultimately who I become.

Your poison is someone's elixr.

Reality begins with imagination.

I am nothing but an atom dancing to universe's tunes.

Death

The dying soldier told the sage- "History only
remembers those who dare."

The sage replied- Indeed.. Indeed.. But to truly live is
to dare.

<u>Death be Proud</u>

The idea of death, in a mysterious way, pushes me
towards life.

Because there is no meaning to life without the
concept of death. That constant fear of uncertainty...
That is what makes me feel alive.

There is only one truth- Death.

Everything else is mere illusion.

Would there be any meaning to life without the fear of
death?

Would there be meaning to anything good if there was
nothing bad?

Is death scared of God or is God scared of death?

What if the last dance lasts forever?

Coming of the Dead

Would the dead want to come back to the living?

Or are they too engrossed in their eternal sleep?

Life is the death of- death.

So is life scared of death or is death scared of life?

Death is peaceful.

Life is chaos.

Yet the truth my friend is- sometimes we all love a
little bit of chaos.

The-God

Darkness

If God can produce light merely by saying 'Let there be light', why is there so much darkness everywhere? Asked the six-year-old boy looking at the night sky?

His father smiled to himself and replied- Would the stars look so beautiful without the darkness behind?

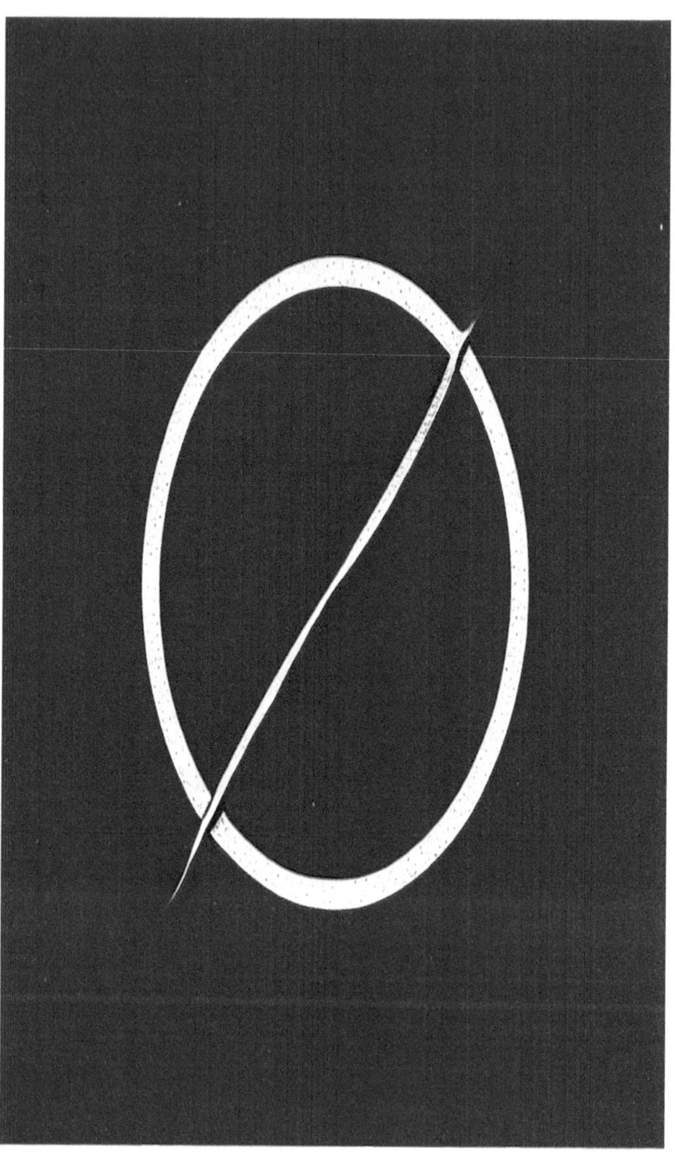

Often people believe God to be an irrational and unscientific idea.

But in reality, God is the only hope that science is true.

The- Devil doesn't come with a red face and two
horns.

He generally comes in a white silk robe and tells the
world- I am God.

To know God is to find beauty in everything.

Including finding beauty in ugliness.

It often gets lost in the complexities of existence.

But truth, love and God are mere synonyms.

All you need to have is- faith!

And hope for the best.

The God is formless and nameless.

The act of naming God- God is the greatest irony.

It is the greatest tyranny.

But this tyranny is our only hope.

The-God

The God lives within each one of us.

And each one of us lives within The God.

God is the greatest truth.

At the same time,

God is the greatest lie that civilization has created.

Yes! The- God is a paradox.

The kingdom of God is right here, right now.

But as Einstein said, 'there is no now in the physical world.'

It exists in the realm of consciousness.

<u>Life</u>

To find meaning in existence is to search for God.

And to live is to endure to become God,

and die!

God is truth.

But the truth is a paradox.

Whole of creation is the mirror of God where life and
death are staring at each other.

The entire point is in order to live, you have to believe in something.

You have to take that leap of faith.

There is no other way.

But what you choose, the choice is yours.

So, I choose to believe in God.

THE END.

Book Description

What if everything you know about existence is both true and false? ***Infinite Nothingness*** is a profound and evocative collection of flash literature that defies the boundaries of time, thought, and tradition. A bold fusion of **mysticism and existentialism, spirituality and absurdity,** this work distills the human experience into concise, thought-provoking reflections.

Drawing from Rumi's wisdom, Kabir's spirit, Nietzsche's fire, Dostoevsky's depths, Tolstoy's soul, Sartre's doubt, Camus's defiance, Shakespeare's grandeur, and Donne's wit, **it's a world where paradox reigns.**

Each piece in Infinite Nothingness acts as a mirror—**reflecting life's beauty, contradictions,** and hidden truths. It **explores identity,** the **search for meaning,** and the **cosmic absurdity of existence.** It moves seamlessly from metaphysics to epistemology, from the divine to the void, **forcing us to confront the paradoxes of self and society.**

What does it mean to be human? To seek meaning in an indifferent universe? To dance between light and darkness? To ponder God, death, love, and the comforting lies of civilization?

For **those who question existence** in the dead of night, **for seekers of wisdom** beyond reason, for **lovers of literature** that disturbs and enlightens—**this is your book.**